NATIONS OF NORTH AMERICA

SEMINOLE

THOMAS KINGSLEY TROUPE

A Lighthouse Book

SEAHORSE PUBLISHING

Teaching Tips for Caregivers:

As a caregiver, you can help your child succeed in school by giving them a strong foundation in language and literacy skills and a desire to learn by reading.

Reading for pleasure and interest will help your child to develop reading skills and will provide the opportunity to practice these skills in meaningful ways. Use the following strategies.

- Encourage the student to read independently at home.
- Encourage the student to practice reading aloud.
- Encourage activities that require reading.
- Establish a regular reading time.
- Have the student write questions about what they read.

Teaching Tips for Teachers:

Engage students throughout the reading process by asking questions.
Sample responses are provided.

Before Reading

- **What do I know about the Seminole?**
  I know that Osceola was the name of one of the Seminole tribe leaders.
  I know that the Seminole live in Florida.
- **What do I want to learn about this topic?**
  I want to learn where the Seminole once lived in Florida. Did they live in the Everglades?
  I want to find out if Seminoles hunted alligators.

During Reading

- **I'm curious to know...**
  I'm curious to know more about the wars fought between the U.S. and the Seminole.
  I'm curious to know more about how Seminoles and African Americans became friends and started to live together.
- **How is this like something I already know?**
  I know that corn, beans, and squash were grown by many Native Americans.
  I know that many enslaved people escaped and tried to find a place to be free.

After Reading

- **What was the author trying to teach me?**
  I think the author was trying to teach me that the Seminole were peaceful people.
  I think the author was trying to teach me that Seminoles are smart and resourceful people who learned how to survive in the swampy Florida Everglades.
- **How did the photographs and captions help me understand more?**
  I learned how people could hide in mangrove trees.
  I learned what Seminole patchwork looks like.

TABLE OF CONTENTS

On the cover: Long ago, Seminole canoes could be up to 30 feet (nine meters) long and could carry an entire family and its possessions through the wetlands. Long poles were used for steering. Poles with sharp ends, or gigs, could be used to spear frogs and fish along the journey.

CHAPTER 1: THE SEMINOLE NATION

A canoe glides through the swamp. One man holds a torch while the other stands ready with a spear. The torchlight shines on an alligator, and the hunter strikes.

Enslaved people manage to escape. They find a safe village of raised houses deep in the **wetlands**. They are welcomed and fed.

A boy looks forward to seeing his cousins at the Green Corn Dance this summer.

At an art fair, craftspeople display handmade dolls with bright patchwork skirts.

What do these stories have in common? They are all part of the proud history of the people of the Seminole Nation.

CHAPTER 2: SEMINOLE HOMELANDS

People in the Seminole Nation are Native Americans. Hundreds of years ago, they were part of the Creek tribe. Some Creek people wanted to go their own way and live in peace. People from other tribes joined them. They formed a new tribe known as the Seminole.

Creek houses were built around a town square.

REGIONS

Creek homelands were on land that would become Georgia and Alabama. When some people left to form the Seminole Nation, they went southeast. They made their homes in swampy wetlands that would become the state of Florida.

Unlike many Native American people, the Seminole did not move from place to place throughout the year. They stayed in one area to farm and hunt.

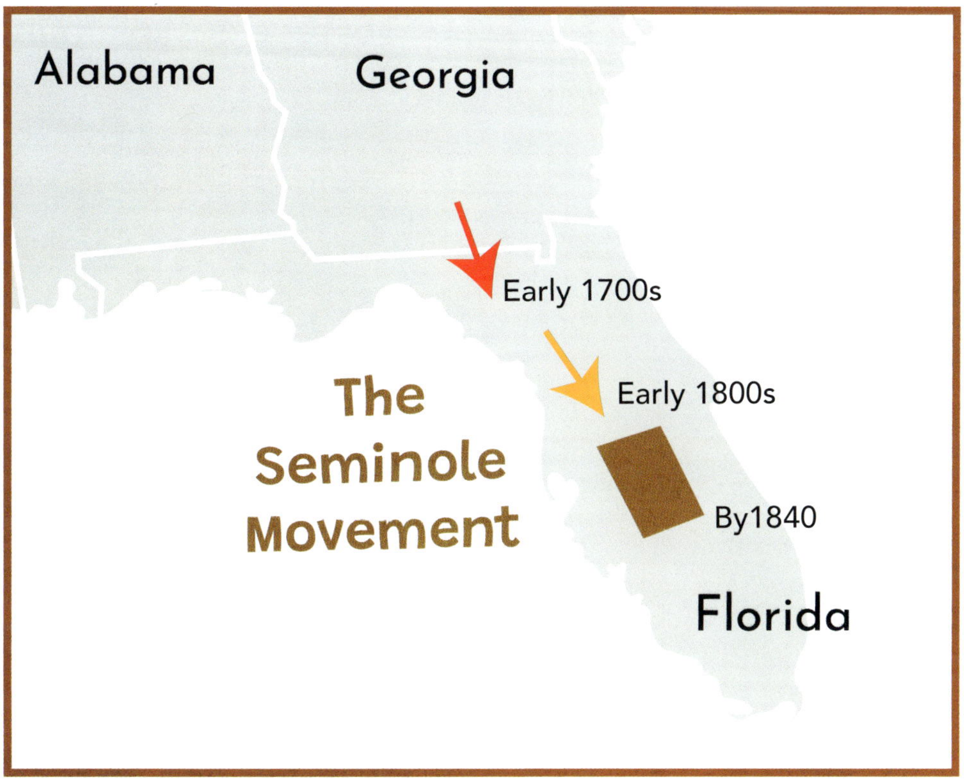

The word *Seminole* comes from the Creek word *simanó-li*, which means "separatist" or "runaway." It may also be related to the Spanish word *cimarron*, meaning "unconquered."

THE STRUGGLE FOR LAND

More than 300 years ago, the Seminole built villages on land that is now the **Florida Everglades**. They hoped the swampy area would keep away outsiders who wanted to control them. Soon, they were joined by other Native Americans, by people from Africa, and by African Americans. Some came to escape **enslavement** by white people. The Seminole welcomed them.

Peace did not last. European **settlers** moved in. During three Seminole Wars, the United States government invaded Seminole lands. They captured those who had run away from enslavers.

During the Seminole Wars, U.S. soldiers took land and burned villages.

Beginning in 1831, more than 100,000 Native Americans, including many Seminole, were forced to leave their homes. They were driven west to land that would become the state of Oklahoma. Many people suffered and died on the way. The journey came to be known as the Trail of Tears.

Seminole people took shelter in wetlands to avoid capture by the U.S. military. Some hid among mangrove trees.

The Seminole fought to defend their homes. But they did not win the wars. Most Seminole people were driven away and forced to move to Oklahoma. A few stayed and hid in Florida's deep swamps.

CHAPTER 3: TRADITIONAL SEMINOLE WAYS OF LIFE

Long ago, the land provided everything the Seminoles needed to live.

After European settlers brought farm animals to the continent, the Seminole began to raise them. Cattle and hogs provided meat. Like other Native Americans, though, they avoided drinking milk as it made them sick.

FOOD

A Seminole hunter

The Seminole were farmers. They planted the three main crops that other Native American tribes grew: beans, corn, and squash. They added pumpkins and other vegetables. They gathered wild rice and mushrooms, too.

Seminole people also fished and hunted wild **game**. They found turkeys, rabbits, turtles, frogs, and alligators. There was always something different to eat.

SHELTER

Before the Seminole left the Creek tribe, they lived in wattle and daub houses. Wattle is sticks and logs woven together with branches and vines. Daub is mud and clay used to cover the sticks. The roofs were cane mats held together with grass.

The Seminole word *chickee* means "house." When they moved into the swamps, the Seminole built chickee stilt houses. These were made of wooden posts and had no walls. The roof was made of **palmetto** leaves. The floor was a platform that was often raised several feet above the wet ground.

A wattle and daub house—with its thick, sturdy walls—would be too hot for life in the Florida Everglades.

LANGUAGE

Like the Creek, the Seminole speak a language that is part of the Muskogean language family. Maskókî and Mikisúkî are two different **dialects**. People in both Florida and Oklahoma speak Maskókî, but Mikisúkî is only spoken in Florida.

The language is difficult to learn. It is very different from English. Words are not traditionally written down. Today, not many people use Maskókî or Mikisúkî. Some people are working to teach them to young people.

Florida Place Names from Mikisúkî	Translation
Apalachicola	place of the ruling people
Chattahoochee	marked stones
Hialeah	prairie
Immokalee	my camp
Miami	that place
Ocala	spring
Palatka	ferry crossing
Yeehaw	wolf
Pahokee	grassy water
Apopka	potato eating place
Okeechobee	big water
Homosassa	pepper place
Thonotosassa	flint place

Six languages from the Muskogean family are still spoken today. They include Alabama, Chickasaw, Choctaw, Creek-Seminole (Maskókî), Koasati, and Mikisúkî.

For many years, Native American children could speak only English at school. In 1990, a law called the Native American Languages Act was passed to help protect tribal languages.

FAMILY AND SOCIETY

Seminole children are born into their mother's **clan**. Traditionally, clans were like big extended families. People could not marry members of their own clan. A husband lived with his wife's clan.

In Seminole families, men **tilled** the soil, and women tended the crops. Women were in charge of households. Men were responsible for hunting and protection. Children learned from adults in their clan. They helped with chores and played games.

Traditionally, the Seminole Nation is matriarchal. This means that women are the heads of their households.

Seminole women often wear many strands of brightly colored beads around their necks. Their bead collections can weigh as much as 12 pounds (five kilograms).

Traditionally, Seminole people are skilled at sewing clothes. By the year 1900, it is said that there was a sewing machine in every chickee. Men, women, and children wore patchwork skirts, shirts, and tunics with bands of brightly colored cotton fabric.

CHAPTER 4: TRADITIONAL SEMINOLE CREATIONS

Long ago, the Seminole made the things they needed from natural materials.

BASKETS

Traditionally, Seminole women wove beautiful baskets from palmetto leaves, pine needles, and **sweetgrass**. The baskets were used to collect food. Today, these handcrafted baskets are valuable works of art.

PATCHWORK

Patchwork is the art form the Seminole are most famous for. It uses colorful strips of fabric sewn together in amazing patterns. Traditional designs represent fire, rain and storm, mountain, and other things from nature.

Dolls made by the Seminole people are palmetto husks stuffed with cotton. The dolls have traditional Seminole clothing and hairstyles. They are popular collector's items.

WEAPONS

Long ago, the Seminole made a variety of weapons. The tomahawk was a small hatchet with a stone head. It was used for striking during up-close battles. War clubs were also used to fight other tribes and settlers.

Bows and arrows were used for battles and for hunting. Blow guns fired small darts. These were good for hunting birds and other small animals. Spears were better for hunting alligators and other large game.

tomahawk

spearfishing

Once, Seminoles made dugout canoes by burying a cypress log in the mud for up to two years. Then, fire was used to burn out the center and axes were used for shaping. Finished canoes had upturned bows to help them cut through sawgrass in the swamp.

CHAPTER 5: SEMINOLE LEADERS

Throughout history, great Seminole leaders have united their people and defended their way of life.

Seminole leader Addie Billie (1884 to 1994) worked to improve the lives of her people.

OSCEOLA (1804 TO 1838)

Osceola was not a chief, but he was an important Seminole leader. He was a respected speaker and warrior. In 1835, he was asked by the U.S. government to sign a **treaty** to move his people off their land. He refused and stabbed a knife into the paper. A war came soon after.

Osceola and his people fought the U.S. Army for two years. When he was asked to meet for peace talks, Osceola was captured. He was sent away to prison where he died a year later.

Seminole men earn their names as teenagers. The man shown here was given the name Asén Yahola. Asén is a ceremonial drink. Yahola is the cry of the wolf. English speakers mispronounced the name and called him Osceola.

ABIAKA (ABOUT 1760 TO ABOUT 1860)

Abiaka was a Seminole spiritual leader. Like Osceola, he didn't want to accept U.S. government demands to leave tribal land. Abiaka wanted his people to stay and fight for their homes.

The U.S. Army hunted Abiaka, but he refused to surrender. When the government wanted to discuss peace, Abiaka stayed away. But he spied on the soldiers' camps. That helped him lead about 300 Seminoles deep into the wetlands, away from settlers. Seminole people survived in Florida because of him.

It was not easy to escape from U.S. soldiers. Fort Picolata, shown here, prevented people from crossing the Saint Johns River in Florida.

A statue of Abiaka leading women and children away from danger stands near the Ah-Tah-Thi-Ki Museum in Florida. *Ah-Tah-Thi-Ki* means "a place to learn."

CHAPTER 6: THE SEMINOLE PEOPLE TODAY

There are about 30,000 Seminole people living in the U.S. today. Many live in Florida or Oklahoma. The group of 300 people who stayed with Abiaka in Florida long ago has grown to a population of thousands.

A modern Seminole woman honors the traditions of her ancestors by wearing beads and a bun hairstyle.

Reservations are like separate countries within the U.S. They have their own governments, police, and services. People who live there are members of their tribes and citizens of the United States.

You can stay at the Guitar Hotel on a Seminole Indian Reservation in Hollywood, Florida. It is owned by the Seminole Tribe of Florida.

RESERVATIONS

Though they can live anywhere, many Seminole people choose to live on **reservations**. There are six Seminole reservations in Florida. Tribal councils there run citrus farms, museums, hotels, and other businesses.

Seminole people in Oklahoma do not have a reservation, but many live in Seminole County. They include the families of African Americans who joined the tribe in Florida hundreds of years ago.

HONORING THEIR HERITAGE

Modern Seminole people have ordinary modern lives. But they remember their tribal heritage. Children are taught the history of their proud ancestors. Many people learn old ways to hunt, fish, and cook. They keep traditions alive.

Families gather at tribal festivals each year. There, they might participate in the ceremonies and dances of their people. This helps them remember that they are part of the proud Seminole Nation of North America.

A Native American mother and her child enjoy the playground on a Seminole Indian Reservation near Tampa, Florida.

Each year, a Green Corn Dance is held in southern Florida. At this spiritual ceremony, Seminole people give thanks, meet with their clans, and participate in stomp dancing.

GLOSSARY

clan (klan): a large group of families descended from a common ancestor

dialects (DYE-uh-lekts): ways that a language is spoken in a particular place or among a particular group of people; different forms of the same language

enslavement (in-SLAYV-muhnt): a system of holding people as prisoners and forcing them to work without wages

Florida Everglades (FLOR-uh-duh EV-ur-glades): a very large area of southern Florida with marshy land, tall grasses, and many swamps

game (game): wild animals that are hunted for food

palmetto (pal-MET-oh): a kind of palm tree that grows in the southern United States and that has leaves shaped like fans

reservations (rez-ur-VAY-shuhnz): areas of land set aside by the government for ownership by Native American tribes

settlers (SET-luhrz): people who make their homes in a new place and who sometimes invade and oppress Indigenous peoples who originally lived there

sweetgrass (SWEET-gras): a slender, sweet-smelling grass that typically grows in very moist soil

tilled (tild): dug up soil and prepared it for planting crops

treaty (TREE-tee): a written agreement between two nations

wetlands (WET-landz): areas where there is a lot of moisture in the soil and where many water plants and creatures make their homes; swamps, bayous, and marshes

INDEX

COMPREHENSION QUESTIONS

1. What type of land did the Seminole people live on?
   a. mountains
   b. deserts
   c. swamps

2. True or False: There are 17 Seminole reservations in Florida.

3. A ________ is a small hatchet weapon with a stone head.
   a. rock club
   b. tomahawk
   c. woodchuck

4. True or False: Osceola slammed his fist into the treaty he did not want to sign.

5. What art form are Seminoles most famous for?
   a. patchwork
   b. jewelry
   c. pottery

Answer Key: 1. c 2. False 3. b 4. False 5. a

ABOUT THE AUTHOR

Thomas Kingsley Troupe is the author of over 200 books for young readers. When he's not writing, he enjoys reading, playing video games, and investigating haunted places with the Twin Cities Paranormal Society. Otherwise, he's probably taking a nap or something. Thomas lives in Woodbury, Minnesota, with his two sons.

Written by: Thomas Kingsley Troupe
Design by: Under the Oaks Media
Series Development: James Earley
Editor: Kim Thompson

Photo credits: LOC: cover; LOC: p. 1, LOC: p. 4; LOC: p. 4; LOC: p. 5; Susanvineyard: p. 5; LOC: p. 6; LOC: p. 7; LOC: p. 8; LOC: p. 9; Laurel A Egan: p. 10; Reading Room 2020: p. 11; RodClement: p. 12; LOC: p. 14-15; Lebrecht Music : p. 17; Michele and Tom Grimm: p. 18; LOC: p. 20; LOC: p. 21; LOC: p. 22; LOC: p. 24; 2018 Sunshower Shots: p. 25; M&N: p. 26;

Library of Congress PCN Data
Seminole / Thomas Kingsley Troupe
Nations of North America
ISBN 978-1-6389-7992-0 (hard cover)
ISBN 979-8-8873-5051-6 (paperback)
ISBN 979-8-8873-5110-0 (EPUB)
ISBN 979-8-8873-5169-8 (eBook)
Library of Congress Control Number: 2022943811

Printed in the United States of America.

Seahorse Publishing Company
seahorsepub.com

Published in the United States
Seahorse Publishing
PO Box 771325
Coral Springs, FL 33077

SEAHORSE PUBLISHING